G000113698

WHY DON'T YOU...

[RE]DESIGN CHRISTMAS?

Big thanks to all the designers for their input on this project, and to our co-elves at [re]design - Olly, Sanjay and Tina - for ensuring that this book went to print in time for Christmas!

And to our parents, thanks for the messy, inspiring, creative fun we had making on the kitchen table...

Sarah and Jason
[re]design

ISBN: 978-0-9557129-3-7
Copyright 2010 Redesigndesign Limited
Published by Redesigndesign Limited t/a [re]design

[re]design
1 Summit Way, Crystal Palace, London SE19 2PU, England, UK

www.redesigndesign.org

All rights reserved. No part of this book may be reproduced in any form without written permission from the publisher.

PREFACE BY BARBARA CHANDLER

I've so enjoyed looking through the projects in this book, and may well end up making some of them. Or at any rate, my older grandchildren will. Years ago – well, 36 years to be precise - I wrote a book called Flat Broke. It was – obviously! – for people in flats who were broke. Many pages were devoted to doing things yourself to save money – learning simple woodworking and decorating skills, for example, and crafts like crochet, knitting, macramé, dyeing and so on. Things were rescued enthusiastically from skips. There was design input from the art students' rooms we photographed. And lots of crates, boxes and packaging were used for furniture, and old clothes for rugs and pieces of patchwork which I have to this day. There was even a coffee table made of soap cartons. But eco-terms such as recycling had not even been invented. The driving forces were saving money, and kitting out somewhere unique to live.

This book is very much in the Flat Broke tradition. But now the motivations are environmental as well as a wish to save money and make something personal. And the involvement of practising designers adds that touch of professional panache. This is another cracking Sarah-and-Jason venture which cannot help but succeed. So have a happy and creative Christmas, with a resolution maybe to make more stuff yourself in the New Year.

With love from Barbara

Barbara Chandler is a photographer, and writes on design for the London Evening Standard and for Homes & Gardens magazine

www.barbarachandler.co.uk

follow me on www.twitter.com/sunnyholt

IMPORTANT: READ BEFORE YOU BEGIN

All Make-It-Yourself activities carry a risk of injury to yourself and others.

The projects in this book are intended for competent adults.

Your safety is your own responsibility, and you use the instructions, plans and suggestions offered at your own risk. You remain responsible for the selection and use of tools, materials and methods.

Before embarking on any of the projects in this book you should satisfy yourself that you are qualified and able to take on the task, and check the suitability of your materials and the appropriateness of your tools.

Some of these projects call for the use of tools that can be highly dangerous if not used properly in an appropriate environment with adequate safety equipment.

Keep in mind that wrong assembly could lead to personal injury or damage, so take care now!

Anyone can use these designs for their personal use. For permission on any sort of commercial application please contact the relevant designer either directly or through [re]design.

Please upload photos of finished projects to www.redesigndesign.org/gallery

CONTENTS

INTRODUCTION

Welcome to [re]design's festive Make It Yourself book.

You will find inside 33 lovely design projects that will make the world a wee bit better this Christmas and make you, your friends and family smile.

The activities range from traditional seasonal craft activities with a designer twist, to innovative techniques that will be new to the most experienced maker.

[re]design reckon that Make It Yourself is intrinsically good. It brings a great sense of satisfaction and pride to the maker, and the emotional investment and personal touch in handmade objects is much appreciated by gift recipients.

Make It Yourself also brings creative opportunities for utilizing household waste locally, encouraging us to look differently at the objects we discard every day. And in using what would otherwise be wasted, we can give more for less.

So this year, instead of traipsing around the shops for all your decorations and presents, have a look in here first. You just might find that there are projects in here that you can make your own, that will make your home lift your spirits and make your loved ones feel, well, loved!

This is the start of your MIY revolution!

Have a fun and thrifty Christmas.

With warmest winter wishes from Sarah and Jason xx

BALLOON BOWLS
GITTA GSCHWENDTNER

Now, you're going to have to take a bit of a leap of faith here when we tell you that these decorative balloon bowls look soooo gorgeous in glorious technicolour! Brightly coloured balloons on the inside, dark sawdust on the outside. This is very posh balloon papier-mâché at its best.

[These bowls are completely biodegradable]

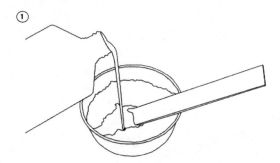

BALLOON BOWLS

Skill Level
●●●○○

Time
3 hours

YOU WILL NEED

Tools: Mixing bowl, Spoon, Spatula, Scissors

Materials: Sawdust, Natural latex liquid, Natural latex balloons, Pigments (optional)

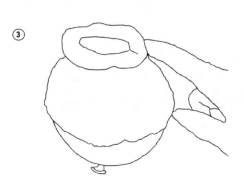

HOW TO MAKE

1 Mix sawdust with latex to achieve a consistency of quite dry porridge. Add pigments or dye as desired.

2 Paste the mixture onto a partially inflated latex balloon. The balloon needs to be quite soft, otherwise it will be too thin and stretched.

3 Create a foot-ring at the bottom of the bowl with a sausage of the mixture.

4 Once the latex mix has dried pop the balloon and cut away excess balloon material.

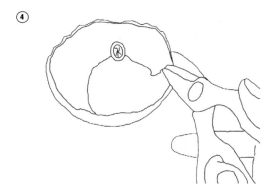

BATTERSEA POWER STATION CROSS STITCH

MAKE INDUSTRIES

Make Industries has a distinctive, modern take on the traditional art of cross stitch. No flowers or teddies here! Delight in the Deco architecture of Battersea Power Station.

[
Cross stitch is the new knitting - jump on the band wagon! It's very easy and has ditched it's frumpy image with new patterns available for today's hip urban crowd.
]

BATTERSEA POWER STATION CROSS STITCH

Skill Level	Time	Template
●●○○○	2 hours	Page 75

YOU WILL NEED

Tools: Embroidery needle, Scissors

Materials: 14 ct White Aida fabric 8x12 cm, Embroidery floss (4 colours), Blank card, Double-sided sticky tape

HOW TO MAKE

1 Find the fabric centre by folding it in four. There is no right of wrong side.

2 Next, find the centre of the pattern chart and pick the first colour that you are going to start with.

3 Don't make a knot art the start or end of a cotton length. At the start keep the ends slightly longer and secure by covering with one or two stitches. At the end of the cotton pass the needle back through the back of a few previous stitches.

4 Form the cross stitches as shown in the illustrations, working in one area of colour at a time. Start in the middle and make sure that all the stitches are formed in the same direction with an even tension to give a neater finish.

5 Any embroidery detail can be added on top of the finished cross stitch, using one strand for light colours and two for darker ones. Make sure you use the fabric holes and secure the thread at the back.

6 When the piece is completed wash in warm water if required and iron on the reverse side.

7 Finally, you can mount your finished work in a card frame. You will need to trim the edges to fit. Place the embroidery behind the window and secure with double-sided sticky tape. Then fold the wing of the card behind the embroidery and secure on the inside with tape.

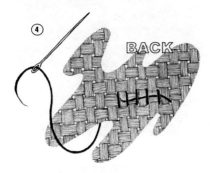

Anchor thread colours

1080	1008	904	382
□	▨	■	■

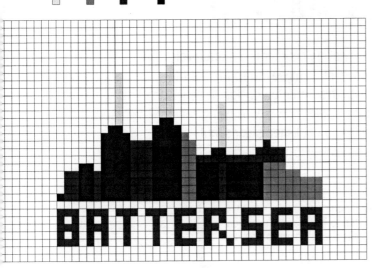

BOTTLETOP CUFFLINKS
TOM MACHIN

The charity shop jewellery counter is not often very inviting, but you could bring those tatty cufflinks into use once more with this bottletop design. If beer's not your recipient's tipple, how about going for a walk with a magpie eye - polished stones, nuts and twigs could all be employed to make quirky cufflinks.

[
This nice little weekend recycling project is fun to make and means your jewellery gift doesn't have to cost the earth.
]

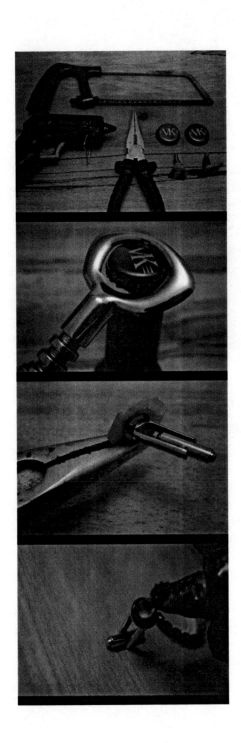

BOTTLETOP CUFFLINKS

Skill Level
●●●○○

Time
40 min

YOU WILL NEED

Tools: Pliers, Small hacksaw, Glue gun

Materials: Old/ broken cufflinks, Bottletops x 2 (these should be removed from bottles gently, easing them off from all sides so not to damage them), Glue sticks or two part epoxy glue, Fine wet and dry sandpaper (240 grit or higher)

HOW TO MAKE

1 Take the old cufflink and carefully remove the top part. Use pliers and/or the hacksaw dependant on its style.

2 Carefully sand all the sharp edges off the side of the bottle tops using the sandpaper, taking care not to scratch the paint. Sand the top surface of the old cufflink too as this will help the glue to stick.

3 Apply enough glue to cover the top of the cufflink and press this firmly to the underside of the bottle top.

BIRTY

EMMA BERRY

It's a bag made from a skirt! Nifty eh? And not too much sewing either. You'll be eyeing up the charity shop isles in a different way next time you're out. Think pleats!

[
Put the swing back into an old skirt with a Birty! Whether it's a stylish handbag or sizable shopping bag, don't let that retro styling go to waste. Reuse and reduce the need for virgin materials.
]

BIRTY

Skill Level   Time
●●○○○   1 hour

YOU WILL NEED

Tools: Needle and thread, Sharp scissors, Pinking shears (optional), Sewing machine (optional), Ruler or measuring tape, Pen or chalk for marking, Pins, Iron

Materials: Old skirt (a pleated one is best)

HOW TO MAKE

1 Take an old skirt.

2 Turn it inside out and lay it flat (you may need to iron it first). Decide how big or small you want your Birty to be and mark the same length all the way around the skirt.

3 Use some sharp scissors to chop the skirt to the right size.

4 Pin the front and back together close to the bottom edge.

5 Sew up the bottom, with a machine if you have one, if not, sew it by hand.

6 Use pinking shears to stop the bottom from fraying (optional).

7 Turn your Birty inside out and use the excess to make a strap. Ta daa, your Birty is complete!

TIPS:

Use the style and features of the skirt to enhance your bag. Turn skirt pockets into secret compartments, add spare buttons as decoration, use pleats to make an expanding bag.

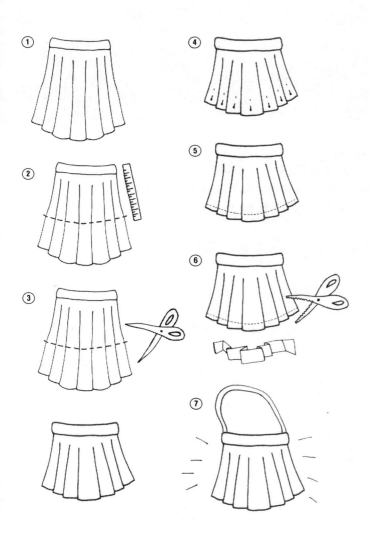

BLIZZARD JAR

LIV BARGMAN
ILLUSTRATION

Now you've got some justification for opening that tin of Christmas chocolates early?. Your wrappers will come in very handy when making these cute thrifty snow domes. What a sweet idea...

[This little Make It Yourself Crimbo snow globe activity can be customised in a multitude of ways and utilises leftovers that would otherwise be part of the excess waste made at Christmas. It can also be used as an unusual and personal gift for somebody. Plus glitter is awesome. As are jam jars.]

BLIZZARD JARS

Skill Level ●●●○○ **Time** 1 hour

YOU WILL NEED

Tool: Pens, Scissors/craft knife, Glue, Paintbrush, Jug

Materials: Jam jar, Plastic object - e.g. toy from a cracker, tree decoration, old brooch, Glycerine (optional, find in your supermarket's cake-making section), Plasticine or modelling clay, Water, Paper or Photo (optional), Acrylic paint (optional), 'Snow' Glitter, any combination of: Plastic sweet wrappers, Foil (kitchen or from sweets and other packaging), White or blue eggshells, Craft Glitter

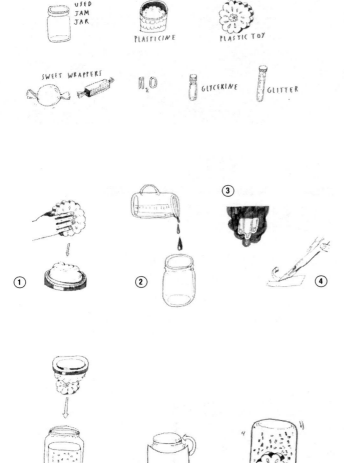

HOW TO MAKE

1 Glue a ball of plasticine into the jar lid. Glue the plastic object into the ball and leave to dry.

2 Meanwhile, fill the jar up with water leaving a slight gap at the top.

3 (Optional) Add 2-3 capfuls of glycerine. This thickens the water so the 'snow' falls and floats around the jar more slowly.

4 Cut sweet wrappers, foil etc. into little pieces to make the glittery 'snow'.

5 Add the glitter snow to the water. Screw the lid on tightly. Glue around the rim of the jar to seal.

6 (Optional) Create a background scene by gluing a drawing, wrapping paper or a photograph around the back of the jar.

7 Tip the jar bottom side up and watch your tiny snowstorm creation.

TIPS:

Wrappers from tins of chocolates are perfect for making into glitter. Use crushed blue or white eggshells for more of a snow stormy look. Cut-up pieces of white plastic bags are also effective. Craft glitter adds delicate sparkles. How about some sequins?

Paint the lid of the jam jar with acrylic paint.

Experiment with different size jars.

You could make little Christmas scenes, or maybe a snowy mountaintop.

CARD CARDS
NIQUENAQUE

These Card Cards are so simple, yet so effective. By taking away the outer layer of corrugated card a lovely new aesthetic is created. Once you've mastered the technique you'll be using it all year round.

[
It's so simple! We don't add anything, just take away, the cardboard's own structure and colour creates the intriguing pattern. And this upcycling method means the material is as recyclable when its done being a card as it was when it was a cardboard box.
]

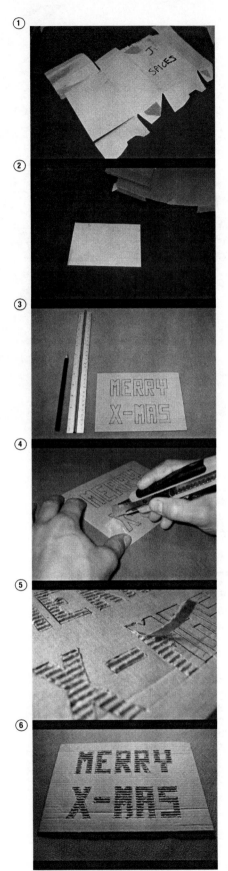

CARD CARDS

Skill Level	Time	Template
●●●○○	30 min	Page 77

YOU WILL NEED

Tools: Craft knife (sharp), Metal ruler, Pencil, Eraser

Materials: An old cardboard box - it must be corrugated, and in good condition.

TIP: Vegetable boxes are great as they often come in lots of wonderful colours.

HOW TO MAKE

1 Find your box and open it out flat.

2 Cut off the side of the box and cut to your intended card size, making sure both sides are clean and crease free.

3 Draw up your edges, and the outlines of the lettering/pattern you intend to put on your card –remember to leave a space between lettering.

TIP: If you are doing many cards then it helps to make a cardboard stencil – a cereal box is perfect for this.

4 With the craft knife cut only the top layer of the card along the outlines of your letters.

TIP: It is quicker to cut all the lines going in the same direction and then rotate the card to do the rest.

5 Using the end of the blade to get under the layer you have cut, gently peel it away, revealing the corrugations underneath. Some cards peel wonderfully easily but others you have to neaten up.

6 Voila! You have your card.

UPLOAD YOUR CREATIONS TO WWW.REDESIGNDESIGN.ORG/GALLERY

CHANGE PURSE
KATE WARD

A knitted plastic bag purse – what a cute use for the plastic shopping bags you will inevitably pick up with some of your impromptu Christmas shopping. Maybe you can make yourself one to keep, say, a few shopping bags in so you're always prepared!

[
These knitted wallets are a fantastic way to use up those pesky plastic shopping bags which seem to accumulate in the back of the kitchen cupboard. The plastic transforms when knitted and feels quite soft, like raffia, yet it is very durable.
]

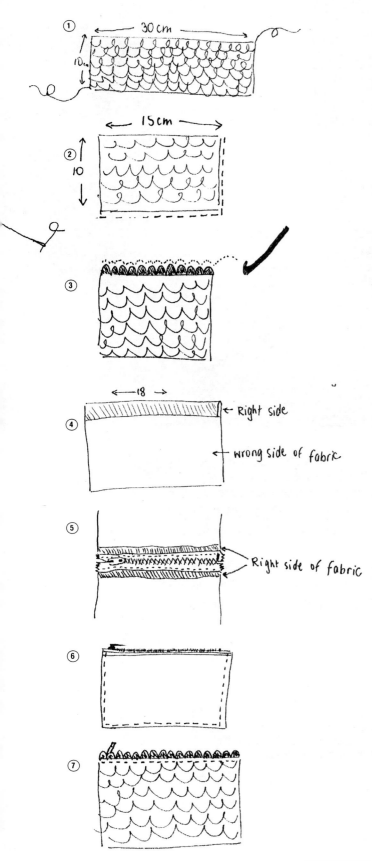

CHANGE PURSE

Skill Level	Time
●●○○○	4 hours

YOU WILL NEED

Tools: 6mm knitting needles, 3mm crochet hook, Wool needle, Regular sewing needle, 33cm x 13cm scrap of fabric for the lining, Zipper

Materials: 2 plastic bags of the main colour, 1 plastic bag for the detailed edge

HOW TO MAKE

1 Cast on 32 stitches and knit 20 rows or until knitting measures 10cm. Cast off.

2 Fold knitting in half lengthwise and sew along bottom and side edge using a strip of recycled plastic bag. Tidy loose ends and turn inside out so that the seams are on the inside.

3 Using a contrasting coloured recycled plastic bag, single crochet into each top stitch to give a neat edge at the opening of the wallet. Tidy loose ends by weaving through the crochet edge. Now might be a good time to have a cup of tea and a biscuit :)

4 (These next steps are the tricky bits) Cut the fabric so that it is slightly bigger than the sewn wallet, then in half so you have two bits of fabric which measure approximately 13 x 18cm. Using an iron press over 1.5cm seam allowance along both bits of fabric.

5 Sew zip onto folded fabric so that the right side of the zip is on the wrong side of the fabric.

6 Fold the fabric in half, making sure to match edges. Sew along edges with a 1.5cm seam allowance.

7 Place lining with zipper inside knitted wallet so that right sides are visible, taking care to match lining seams with knitted seams. Stitch lining into place using thread that matches lining colour (so that your hand stitching is less visible) near the zipper edge.

8 Now you've finished! Fill your wallet with your favourite things and enjoy!

CARDBOARD ARMOUR
SAM HILL DESIGN

A perfect project post-walk on Boxing Day, this armour would look great made from the colourful boxes your Christmas presents came in. En garde!

[
With a cardboard suit you'll never be short of a fancy dress. Put it on display and it'll lend your house a certain medieval class
]

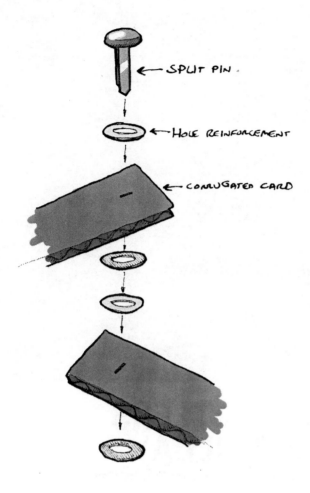

SPLIT PIN

HOLE REINFORCEMENT

CORRUGATED CARD

CARDBOARD ARMOUR

Skill Level	Time	Template
●●●○○	1day	Page 79

YOU WILL NEED

Tools: Measuring tape, Craft knife, Cutting mat, Scissors, Hole punch, Sponge

Materials: Cardboard, Paper, Staples, Paperclips, Gummed tape, Split pins, Self-adhesive hole reinforcements, Self-adhesive velcro, String

HOW TO MAKE

1 Do a bit of research into armour before you start – look up images online for inspiration from throughout history.

2 Gather together lots of cardboard boxes.

3 Take extensive measurements of the body the armour is designed for.

A typical suit of armour consists of ten items: Helmet, Gorget (neck brace), Spaulders (shoulder pads), Rerebrace (arms), Gauntlets, Cuirass (chest plate), Tassets (leg protectors), Cuisses (thighs), Greaves (shins), Sabatons (feet)

4 For the best-fitting suit make paper proto-types of each component, cut quickly with scissors and hold in place with staples or paperclips.

5 Use a sharp scalpel and a cutting mat to cut the cardboard shapes out.

6 Use gummed tape to fix the pieces together. Gummed tape needs moistening to become sticky. In the long run a small sponge is better for wetting the tape than your tongue! For hinged parts use split pins and prevent the cardboard tearing with several hole reinforcements.
TIPS: To help with articulation use 'lames' instead of large pieces of card. Lames are multiple thin strips of solid material that move over each other, loosely attached by perpendicular strips of a more flexible material (like thick paper or thin card). Use string threaded through reinforced holes in the cardboard to tie parts together or onto the wearer. Self-adhesive Velcro strips can be really useful for hidden attachments such as on the gorget. A sword and shield are optional extras!

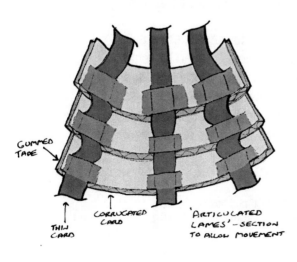

GUMMED TAPE

THIN CARD

CORRUGATED CARD

'ARTICULATED LAMES' – SECTION TO ALLOW MOVEMENT

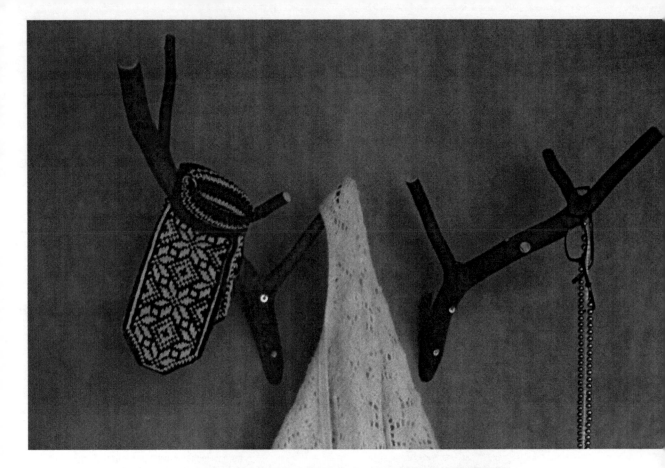

CHESTNUT ANTLERS (FOR MATHILDA)

DUNCAN KRAMER

Do you love anyone enough to make them a pair of these splendid vegan antlers? They'd be regal in the hall storing those warming winter hats and scarves, or beautiful in the bedroom hung with beads and rings. Hmm, maybe you should collect enough wood to make a pair for yourself too.

[Leave the tat in the shops.
Go for a walk in the woods.]

CHESTNUT ANTLERS (FOR MATHILDA)

Skill Level
●●●○○

Time
2 hours

YOU WILL NEED

Tools: Handsaw, Craft knife, Drill, Screwdriver

Materials: Fresh-cut tree branches from a wood, Screws, Glue, Small plywood fillets

HOW TO MAKE

1 Cut some forking branches of green chestnut in a wood and trim them.

2 Add extra branch pegs if needed.

3 Small wood fillets should be added, to give greater fixing strength when later applied to a wall or cabinet.

4 Drill holes, and fix the Chestnut Antlers by screwing, nailing or bolting to a suitable surface.

TIP: Green wood is used because of its strength and the bark can be cut and peeled in any decorative pattern.

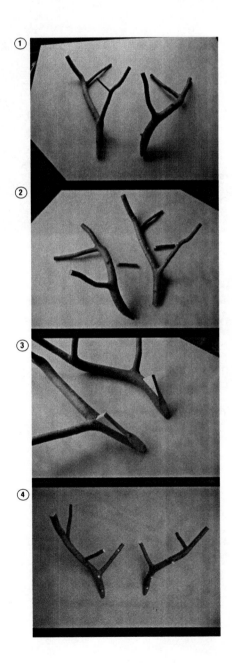

CHRISTMAS COMFORT
LULA DOT

All together now, ahhhh! This speedy make, cuddly design is great for making its recipient feel cosy and loved on a cold winter's night.

[A great way to give a second life to those slightly embarrassing Christmas jumpers]

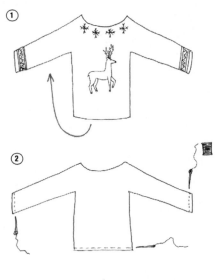

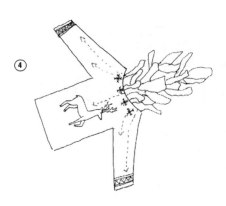

CHRISTMAS COMFORT

Skill Level   Time
●●○○○   30 min

YOU WILL NEED

Tools: Sewing machine or needle and thread

Materials: Jumper, Recycled fabric - old clothes or other material

HOW TO MAKE

1 Take an old jumper and turn inside out

2 Sew closed bottom opening and sleeves

3 Turn jumper the right way round through the neck hole

4 Stuff with recycled fabric

5 Stitch up neck hole

6 Hug

TIP: Place a magnet in the end of each of the sleeves for the full wrap around hugging experience!

EDIBLE DECORATIONS
ANTHONY DICKENS STUDIO

Whether for an extra special touch to your Christmas cake or to hang in your tree, these cute decorations are really rather tasteful, but feel free to add your own colourful twist.

[
You can use the trees with wooden sticks as cake decorations, and the thread trees as decoration for the Christmas tree!
]

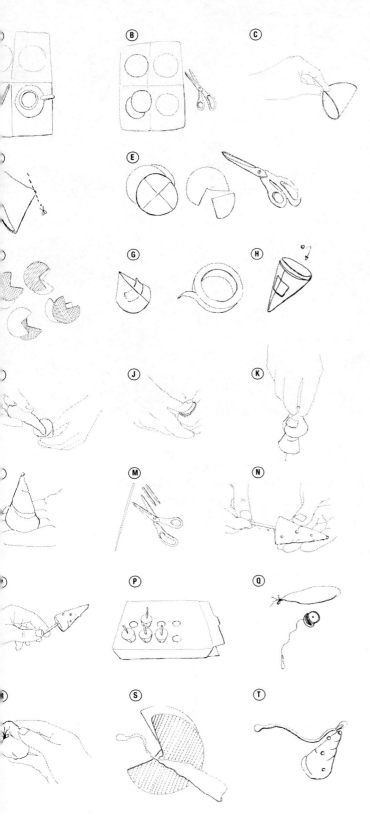

EDIBLE DECORATIONS

Skill Level
●●○○○

Time
1 hour

YOU WILL NEED

Tools: Pencil, Tape, Scissors
Materials: Large sheet of paper, Wax paper, Thread,

Food colouring (if you want green trees), Wooden sticks, Ready rolled icing, Large cup, Silver edible ball decorations, Cereal box

HOW TO MAKE

1 Take a sheet of paper and draw around a cup several times. [A] Cut out the circles with scissors. [B]

2 Fold the circles in half [C] Fold the half circles again and cut off the tip of the triangles. Unfold the paper. [D]

3 Using the centre hole as reference cut out a pie shape from the circles. [E]

4 Repeat steps 1-3 for the wax paper. [F] Roll pairs of wax and white paper into cones (wax paper inside), and use tape to close.[G]

5 Drop a sugar ball in each mould. [H]

6 Shape icing into long strips. Fill the moulds, twisting the dough down. [I]

7 Push gently down the moulds. [J] Then flip the moulds to release trees. [K]

8 Add more silver decorations to the sides of the icing tree. [L]

9 Cut the wooden sticks to make tree trunks. [M] Insert. [N]

10 Place trees back in their paper moulds. [O] Make holes in a cereal box to stand them in and refrigerate for two hours. [P]

11 To make hanging trees, cut, loop and knot a piece of thread. [Q] Squish the knot in some icing. [R]

12 Place the icing with thread on the wax and paper circles. Roll the cone mould, tape and press the dough down. [S]

13 Release from mould, add decorations and leave to dry in the fridge. [T]

FILIGREE FANTASY
PHIONA RICHARDS

This lovely project shows off a simple technique that gives a beautiful effect. Filigree Fantasy would be great both on and under the tree.

[
As a book sculptor I am continually exploring what paper as a material can be used for. This is a beautiful gift for a loved one during the festive season. The hues and tones of the book paper will change with age.
]

FILIGREE FANTASY

Skill Level
●●○○○

Time
1 hour

YOU WILL NEED

Tools: Pens and Candles of different diameters, Paper Shredder, Metal ruler, Craft knife, Cutting mat

Materials: Old books, PVA glue, Cocktail Stick (as glue applicator), Sketch paper, Pen

HOW TO MAKE

1 Sketch down your design on a piece of paper. You need to be thinking Mandala.

2 Take your book apart and shred about 20 pages using your paper shredder. Glue some of the strips end to end to make long strips.

3 Using your design as a guide you need to prepare your coils. To do this you first must select a pen or candle. Wrap one of your long strips around the tool until you run out of paper. Glue the end of the paper in to secure the coil, carefully slide off the end of the tool. Continue in this way using long strips and a variety of tools until you have all the coils to complete your design.

4 You can change the shape of the coils by pressing and pinching. Squashing the coil will give you a petal shape. Pinching the coil at one end will give you a teardrop shape.

5 Once all your shapes are ready assemble by gluing all the coils together using your original design as a guide.

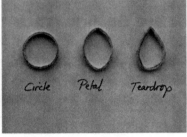

Circle   Petal   Teardrop

IWIRE

SANJAY KATIYAR

The iDock is a neat design to help its user make the most of their iPod, iPhone or iPad. We want lots please! One for the office, one for the bedroom, one for the kitchen, one for the living room, one for the bathroom...

[
With the easy and simple manipulation of a coat hanger you can prop up your iPhone/iPod device at an angle for additional support when viewing the screen.
]

IWIRE

Skill Level
●●●○○

Time
1 hour

YOU WILL NEED

Tools: Pliers, Tape, Ruler, Marker

Materials: Coat hanger, Coat Hanger tips (optional)

HOW TO MAKE

1 Cut the bent sides of the coat hanger.

2 Mark the halfway point on the straight part of the wire.

3 From your midway point measure out 2cm on both sides and bend at a 45 degree angle.

4 Mark out the half way points on the sides shown above.

5 Bend these marked points upwards at a 90 degree angle to achieve the shape shown above.

6 Mark the halfway points shown on the sides illustrated above.

7 Bend at newly marked points.

8 Bend the form inwards so the front is flat when on a surface.

9 Mark out roughly 1cm from the tips and bend these marked areas upwards to achieve the shape as illustrated.

10 Add coat hanger tips (optional) and insert iPhone/iPod.

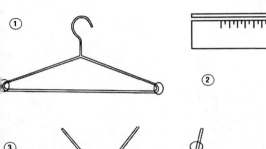

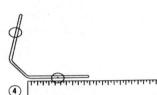

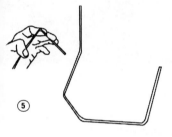

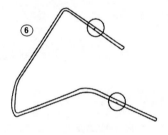

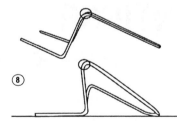

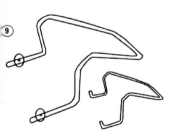

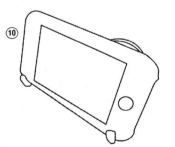

KILIKANZER

ANTIGOR

What is it? An emu relative perhaps? Make yours look as friendly or scary as you like. Maybe when you've mastered this puppet making project you could make the cast for a Christmas puppet pantomime extravaganza.

[
In contrast to buying mass-produced objects, in making your own characterful Kilikanzer from household objects you make a bit of personal history - that is what is valued most.
]

A

SHOPPING BAG

B

EGG BOX

C

D

COTTON

E

SHOPPING BAG

F

G

PING PONG

KNOT

SMASH 3 IT

1. 2.

TIP: When stitching to cardboard premake holes for your needle to go through and make stitches in the same way you stitch a button.

KILIKANZER

Skill Level	Time
●●●●○	2 hours

YOU WILL NEED

Tools: Craft knife, Pins, Ruler, Hammer or Mallet, Bradawl

Materials: Small egg box, Cotton tote shopping bag (an old one is good), 3 Ping-pong balls, 2 Small drink cans, Cotton wool, Needle and thread, Buttons or other decorations, Pair of chopsticks, Matchsticks

HOW TO MAKE

1 Split the cotton bag in two along the edges. [A] Cut the egg box to make the shape of an animal chest. [B]

2 From the neck, sew one half of the bag to the egg box. The handles are the legs – put them in the right place! [C]

3 Stitch from the chest to the end of the bag to creating a triangle tail shape. Stuff with cotton wool. [D]

4 Cut from the other half bag a 10cm wide strip, fold in half and cut off the corners, then stitch the edge. [E]

5 Make a small cut in the middle and turn the head inside out.

6 Fill with cotton wool, then fold in half, stitch the jaws, and add buttons and other bits.

7 Twist some yarn together to make four puppet strings and secure the ends by knotting to a matchstick.

8 Make holes at opposite ends of your ping-pong balls with the bradawl and thread through your head and the ping-pong balls to the body.

9 Find the spot on the body where the weight is balanced and insert stringed matchstick.

10 Cross and secure your chopsticks then attach the head and body strings to the end of one stick. Adjust the length of your strings so your Kilikanzer sits in an upright position.[F]

11 Knot the bottom of each leg. Carefully cut the cans 3.5cm away from the bottom. Place a leg knot insideA each can, then smash the cans, so the legs hold onto it and there are no sharp edges.

12 Find the spot on the body where the weight is balanced and insert stringed matchstick.

13 Attach the remaining two strings to the legs, near the feet, and to the second chopstick. Adjust the length to fit, [G]

LOVELY AND QUIET MUG
SUGRU

Mugs are made pretty and less clattery with the addition of a great new air-drying soft silicone. sugru sticks to pretty much anything so it is wonderful stuff for repairing things and making them fit you better.

[sugru makes your cups lovely and quiet and acts as a beautiful built in coaster, is dishwasher proof and looks great when you are drinking tea.]

LOVELY AND QUIET MUG

Skill Level
●●○○○

Time
30 min

YOU WILL NEED

Tools: Scissors

Materials: Mugs, sugru (a soft-touch, air drying silicone), and sugru colour mixing chart (available from www.sugru.com)

Health and Safety: sugru must not be used where it will have prolonged food contact – so do not use it inside or on the rim of your mug.

HOW TO MAKE

1 Plan your patterns and colours - sugru comes in 4 colours: orange, green, blue and black. You can also create great new colours by mixing them.

2 Get a bunch of mugs (old or new) you will be able to make several sugru coasters with a few sachets of sugru.

3 Give your mugs a good wash and dry them ready for some sugru hacking.

4 Cut open your sugru sachets and mix the colours you want to use for your design. Break each sachet into 3 pieces, this way you can make several colours. Mixing sugru is easy - just knead two colours in your fingers until it is thoroughly blended.

5 To build your pattern, work small - break off a tiny piece of sugru and roll it into a mini sausage.

6 Press the mini sausage gently onto the mug making sure that it is bonded. Repeatedly and gently touch the sugru to adjust the shape until you are happy.

7 Build up your design with small pieces.

8 When you are happy with your design, leave the mug overnight to cure.

9 Have a lovely cup of tea!

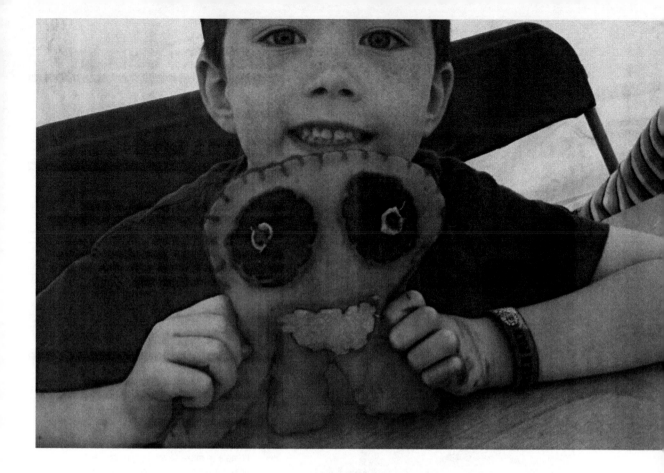

MIMO
WEMAKE

Make the kids in your life their own personalised loveable, huggable monster. Seed their imagination by giving their MIMO a name and special power, and they'll be off on imaginative adventures, returning with stories to share.

[
Don't be sucked into bying the latest fad licensed toy this Christmas, make your own cuddly creation instead.
]

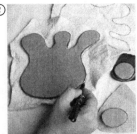
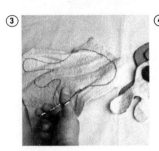
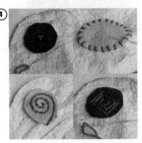
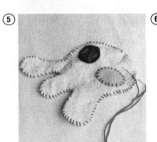

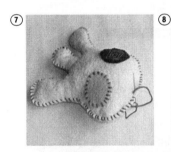

MIMO

Skill Level	Time	Template
●●●○○	2 hours	Page 81

YOU WILL NEED

Tools: Dressmaker's chalk or Pen, Scissors, Embroidery needle

Materials: Well-loved old clothes or blankets, Wool, Card for template

HOW TO MAKE

1 Collect together the bits of material you will need.

2 Cut out template and draw around to mark out two body shapes and two eyes.

3 Carefully cut your body and eyes out.

4 Decorate your eyes. Take one of the body pieces and sew on the eyes.

5 Sew the body shapes together, leaving a 5cm gap for the stuffing at the top.

6 Cut up off-cuts to create stuffing and fill MIMO.

7 Sew up the gap.

8 Make your MIMO unique with crazy hair.

MY PROFILE LAMP
RADA LEWIS

You can follow Rada's magnificent profile to make this beautiful lamp. Or personalise the profile shape to fit the person who lights up your life.

[A great Christmas gift, this design can be personalised and take on other roles as a festive decoration, Valentine or birthday present.]

MY PROFILE LAMP

Skill Level	Time	Template
●●●○○	2 hours	Page 83

YOU WILL NEED

Tools: Pen, Scissors, Double-sided sticky tape

Materials: A4 Paper – preferably reused, LED battery powered lamp (optional)

HOW TO MAKE

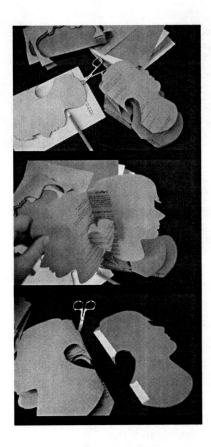

1 Fold a sheet into two along the longer side. Trace out the profile pattern as shown or create your own template.

2 Repeat and make as many elements as you wish (around ten should be about right)

3 Fold out the inner heart shape in the opposite direction to the profile fold.

4 Attach strips of double-side sticky tape as shown.

5 Stick the profiles together to achieve the form.

6 You can attach the form to the wall using double-sided sticky tape. A small LED battery lamp positioned in the inner cavity gives added effect.

TIP: Why not personalise the profile to match the person you are making for.

OCTOPUS ILLUMINATI

ARASH AND KELLY*

Arash and Kelly have been thinking positive during the economic downturn and created a collection of designer lampshades that you can make for free. First seen at the V&A don't you know! The Octopus is our favourite. Visit www.arashandkelly.com to download all three designs.

[Spend time making, hacking, modifying and improving on this lampshade design. Trace the designs and make them at your own pace, with your own hands for your loved ones and friends.]

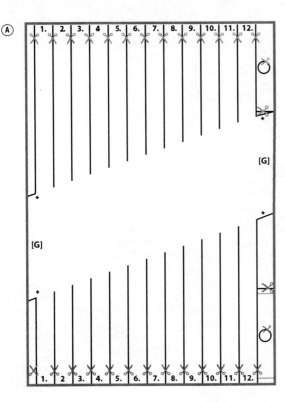

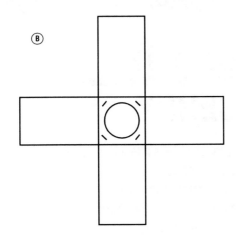

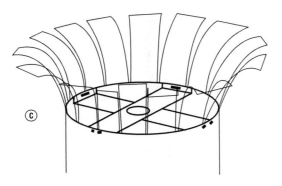

OCTOPUS ILLUMINATI

Skill Level	Time	Template
●●○○○	40 min	Page 85

YOU WILL NEED

Tools: Scissors, Stapler, Ruler

Materials: A1 Paper

Health and Safety: The shade is only for use with energy saving bulbs. Switch off the light before attaching shade.

HOW TO MAKE

1 Cut along all the black lines as indicated. When cutting the 13 strips only go as far as the diagonal line.

2 To create the loops, lay the lightshade flat and curl opposing, identically numbered strips round so that the ends overlap by about 1cm, then staple them (1 to 1, 2 to 2 etc.).

3 To make the cyclinder, punch holes through the crosses, then curl the midsection round - overlapping the ends [G], aligning the holes and securing with split pins.

4 You're almost there! Now, to make the bulb holder, staple the two small pieces with holes together around the hole.

5 Then attach to one of the open ends of the midsection with staples.

TIP: Try using decorative scissors to get a more exciting edge!

*
Many thanks to David Gardener and Jenny Brewer for their help on this project.

UPLOAD YOUR CREATIONS TO WWW.REDESIGNDESIGN.ORG/GALLERY

ODD SOCK TOY
EMMA BERRY

Ms Berry (we should call her that as she's a teacher now you know) has a bit of a thing about odd socks, she doesn't like to see them wasted and reckons that if we all think up some good uses for them the world will be a better, more creative place.

[
Give a sock a home.
]

ODD SOCK TOY

Skill Level   Time
●●○○○   2 hours

YOU WILL NEED

Tools: Needle and Thread, Scissors

Materials: Socks, Buttons

HOW TO MAKE

1 Gather some odd, old or unloved socks.

2 To form the body of your soft toy take one sock, stuff it from toe to top with odd socks and sew up the opening. You can use the heel of the sock to create the nose or face.

3 Take four more socks and chop them off just before the heel. Stuff these in the same way and sew up the openings to form two legs and two arms.

4 Sew them on to the body.

5 Finally, add some old buttons for eyes and sock or other fabric scraps for hair.

6 Hug.

TIPS:

Your odd sock toy could be any shape and size - why not try a caterpillar or an octopus?

Keep the best looking socks for the body, legs and arms and save the holey socks for stuffing.

Don't forget to wash the odd socks first!

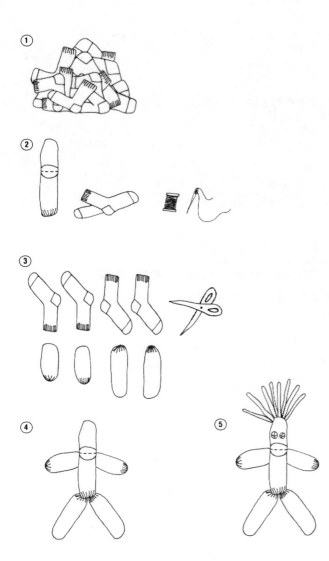

PALLET STOOL
STUDIOMAMA

More guests over for Christmas than you have seats? Collect some pallets and craft a few of these funky stools and you'll all be sitting pretty. Makes a great side table too.

[
The pleasure of making seems to have been forgotten. We have got used to being able to buy more or less everything so cheap that the idea of making anything out of necessity does not make sense anymore. Today the incentive for homemade is much more about environmental issues, social connectivity and the pleasure of making.
]

Preparation of Pallets:

The idea here is deconstruct to reconstruct. Take the pallet apart with your crowbar and hammer or mallet and cut the following components to length:

- 4 seat slats, 350mm high x 87mm wide

- 5 under-seat slats, 310mm high x 62mm wide

- 4 legs, 430mm high x 87 mm wide

- 2 base elements, 310mm high by 87mm wide.

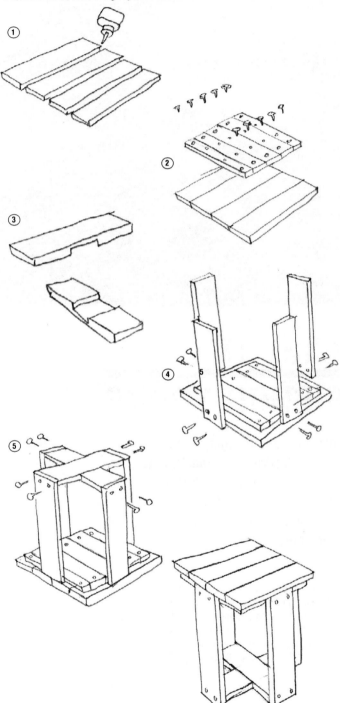

PALLET STOOL

Skill Level	Time
●●●●●	1 day

YOU WILL NEED

Tools: Wood glue, Crowbar, Hammer or Mallet, Saw, 1mm or 2mm drill, Countersink (a drill bit that creates a tapered hole), Chisel

Materials: Wooden pallet, 36 number six 30mm twin-thread wood screws, 6 x 50-60mm nail/screws

HOW TO MAKE

1 Firstly, pre-drill two holes about 2.5cm in from each end of the under seat slats.

2 Carefully pre-drill and countersink two holes at either end of each of the legs. The holes need to be about half the measurement of the thickness of your wood from the edge (ie if your wood is 16mm thick, drill the holes 8mm from the edge of the leg).

3 The two slats at the base of the stool have to be chisel cut to form a flush cross. Use a saw to make five cuts halfway through the thickness of the wood. This makes it easier to chisel the wood out - see illustration.

4 Now you have all your elements prepared and cut to size, glue the sides of the upper seat planks together and leave them to dry.

5 Once the glue has set, screw the under-seat planks on to the centre of the top seat. To give the structure strength.
Fix the two rows of slats in opposing directions - see illustration.

6 Glue the bottom cross of the stool together. This fits together like a Christmas tree foot.

7 The legs are secured between the top seat and the under seat planks, so they are flush with the main seat of the stool. Use wood glue on the end of the legs to help fix them to the seat, then drill the screw through the pre-drilled holes.

8 Fix the base to the legs by gluing the screwing the end of the planks. It is easier to do this with the stool turned upside down

9 Prevent splinters by giving the stool a gentle sand.

UPLOAD YOUR CREATIONS TO WWW.REDESIGNDESIGN.ORG/GALLERY

PIXEL-IT

OLIVER BISHOP-YOUNG

Perfect for compact homes and friendly offices, this range of designs for festive frolics with Post-its is just for starters. Create your own layouts using the grids provided. You could even get clever with a favourite face on the computer; turn up the contrast and lower the dpi to create a Post-it pixel pattern!

[
Decorate your place with minimal effort and stock up on Post-it notes for the New Year at the same time. The notes can be restuck for a constantly changing space before returning to the office after the festive season.
]

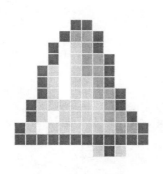

PIXEL-IT

Skill Level	Time	Template
●○○○○	30 min	Page 87

YOU WILL NEED

Tools: Scissors (optional)

Materials: Post-It Notes

HOW TO MAKE

1 You can either start by sticking the Post-It Notes straight to the wall and building your design as you go; or you can use a grid to plan out the design, making sure it will fit in your space. Remember to check the size of your post-it notes, most are 76 x 76 mm but they do vary.

You can use the examples on this page or find examples elsewhere. Two great sources are old cross stitch patterns and retro computer game graphics (sprites).

2 Choose a good place to start placing the notes. For example, if you were making a Christmas tree its best to start from the ground up.

3 Place one note at a time keeping them square to one another and with a consistent gap between them.

One technique is to cut the notes into shapes such as baubles. Just make sure you keep a section of the sticky bit!

Sprites and cross stitch patterns look best when done neatly, following straight grid lines. But don't be afraid to mix up styles of your own. The best way to check how its coming on is to stand back and see the overall view.

TIPS:

If you run out of notes or don't have any in the first place, you can make your own by cutting scrap paper into squares and fixing them with rings of masking tape.

Googles search options are a great way to find sprites. Do an image search for the image you want, eg 'star', and set the image size parameter to 'exactly' and type a number between about 12-36 pixels in both fields.

RECYCLED PLASTIC BAG CHRISTMAS WREATH

GIRLWITHBEADS

With the best of intentions we can't always say no to a plastic shopping bag. girlwithbeads shows how to make a recycled plastic bag Christmas wreath that'll make your neighbours smile.

[A fun, eco-friendly & money-saving idea to keep you occupied during the holidays. I always find that despite refusing bags as much as possible I still end up with drawer full! So be creative with all those plastic bags and be the envy of your friends with a unique home made decoration.]

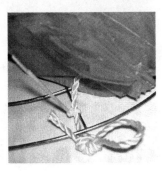

RECYCLED PLASTIC BAG CHRISTMAS WREATH

Skill Level
●●○○○

Time
2 hours

YOU WILL NEED

Tools: Scissors, Bradawl (or other hole-maker)

Materials: 12 inch Circular metal frame (available from florists, ebay, or make your own using a wire coathanger), 15-20 Plastic bags, 1.5 metres of Thick string (or Garden twine), approx 25 Cable ties (or garden wire), blob of Blu-tack

HOW TO MAKE

1. Flatten a plastic bag. Fold it in half lengthways, then in half again. Then concertina fold until you are left with a square.

2. Carefully make hole in centre of the square using bradawl and blu-tack to protect your table.

3. Tie a loop at one end of the string to hang the wreath from.

4. Thread the square of plastic onto the string.

5. Cut through all the folded layers of plastic.

6. Repeat the process to fill the string.

7. At this point you could use the string of plastic bags as tinsel!

8. Lay the string of bags on the metal frame to check you've done enough, then tie ends together.

9. Starting from the loop, attach the string to the frame using the cable ties.

10. Use enough cable ties to secure the wreath firmly into place.

11. Next make a bow from a bag of contrasting colour and attach it with a cable tie from the back.

12. Ta-dah! You can proudly hang up your eco-friendly wreath for all to see.

TIP: You can stick to one colour theme or be more adventurous and use bags in various colours. You could even jazz up your wreath with acrylic paint and glitter.

UPLOAD YOUR CREATIONS TO WWW.REDESIGNDESIGN.ORG/GALLERY

RECYCLED PLASTIC LACE LAMPSHADE

KATE WARD

Flattened plastic bag knitting plus light - wow, what a crafty idea and fabulous effect! The lazy amongst us might try bypassing the knitting stage to see what happens if you just twist, knot and iron the bags. Nowhere near as pretty or predictable but thumbs up for experimenting...

[Using heat to fuse the knitted plastic creates a quirky lace-like lampshade (and once you get the hang of it you could adapt any knitting or crochet pattern) - for me the best bit is discovering the beautiful shadows that are created by the shade, casting delicate patterns of light and dark into the room.]

RECYCLED PLASTIC LACE LAMPSHADE

Skill Level
●●●●○

Time
2 hours

YOU WILL NEED

Tools: Pair of 8mm Knitting needles, Scissors, Iron, Sewing needle, Pegs, Fishing line

Materials: 15 Recycled plastic bags (make sure you don't use bags that are labeled degradable/biodegradable/compostable), Baking paper, Torn or unloved wire frame lampshade with fabric removed

Health and Safety: The shade is only for use with energy saving bulbs. Switch off the light before attaching shade. Be sure to do the ironing in a well ventilated room - melted plastic can be smelly.

HOW TO MAKE

1 Fold plastic bag in half, handles together then half again and cut into 2cm strips. When opening the strips they should be circular. Discard bottom join and handles.

2 Loop circular strips together using slip knots to create a length of yarn and roll into balls.

3 Measure the circumference of the shade - this will be the length you will need to knit. The beauty of this knitting pattern is that you can measure the length as you knit. Remember to allow a 2.5cm seam allowance and that when the knitting is ironed it is no longer flexible or stretchy so it is best to knit an inch more than required. Continue repeating rows 1 - 10 of Lace Pattern until piece measures length required.

4 Place the knitting between two sheets of baking paper and press with a hot iron. The heat and pressure will flatten and fuse the knitting together. Take care not to iron for too long - or you will totally melt your knitting. Allow to cool and gently peel away baking paper. Trim loose ends.

5 Using pegs position the plastic lace around the wire frame taking care to ensure the frame is centered on the knitting. The pegs will help hold the lace in place. The frame should be approximately 2.5cm in from the edge of the knitting. Using clear fishing line, slipstitch top and bottom of the wire frame to the plastic lace. Then remove pegs.

UPLOAD YOUR CREATIONS TO WWW.REDESIGNDESIGN.ORG/GALLERY

REWRAP
TINA DHINGRA

This is a very classy way to use reclaimed paper for Christmas wrapping. Perfect for presenting smaller gifts. Mix newspaper with colourful scraps – lovely!

[
This a clever way to use some geometric patterns to make holiday gift wrapping without utilsing any type of adhesive.
]

REWRAP

Skill Level Time
●●○○○   10 min

YOU WILL NEED

Tools: Scissor, Ruler

Materials: Paper shopping bags, Magazines, Newspaper, Paper scraps

HOW TO MAKE

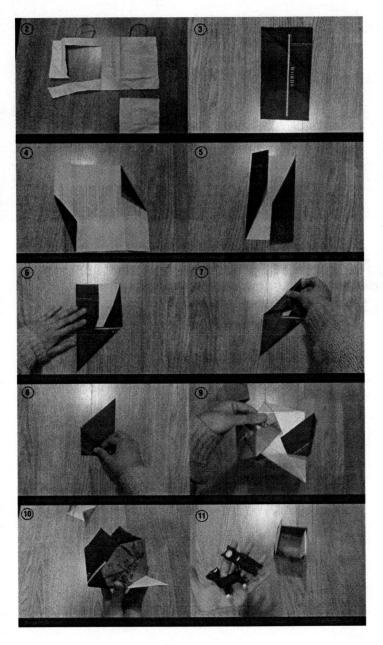

1 Find old shopping bags, magazines, newspapers that have fun images. Choose 6 materials to work with. For the paper bags, peel off the bottom and cut through one of the sides to make into a flat surface.

2 Measure and cut out six squares (21.5cm x 21.5cm). Set 5 of them aside and grab a square to work with.

3 Put the exposed side down. Fold the paper in half and fold that half again. Open up the paper and there should be 3 crease lines going down the paper.

4 Take the bottom left corner and fold it up to the first crease line. Fold that corner once again to the same crease line.

5 Repeat step 4 to the top right corner. And fold into the page on both sides. You will now have a rectangle to work with.

6 Fold the bottom right corner of the rectangle into the first crease line underneath the left flap.

7 Fold the top left corner down into the right side and insert into the flap.

8 Flip the piece around so that the pointed edges are on the left bottom and top right. Fold the pointed edge up so that it forms a triangle, set this piece aside and make 5 more.

9 You're now ready to piece together the box... You'll need two piece and both hands. Have the piece in your left hand vertical and the second piece horizontal. Slot the piece in your right hand into the bottom left corner of the one in your left hand.

10 Repeat the slotting step for 4 of the pieces.

11 Once five of the pieces have been slotted together, gather the gift items and place them in the box. Place the last piece down and place the final set of the pointed corners into the slots.

SANTA UP!
A SECRET CLUB

Have the kids been good for Santa? Get making your own tickly white beard and help keep the magic alive. For more ways to disguise visit www.schhh.org

[The fastest, non-itchiest way to grow facial hairstyles.]

SANTA UP!

Skill Level	Time	Template
●○○○○	30 min	Page 89

YOU WILL NEED

Tools: Craft knife or Scissors, Hole punch

Materials: Thick paper, Ring reinforcers, Elastic band

HOW TO MAKE

1 Cut out.

2 Fold the moustache but down.

3 Punch holes for elastic and attach ring reinforcers for added strength.

4 Add elastic band.

5 Decorate and wear!

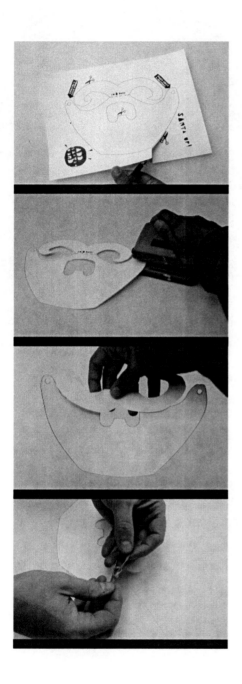

SHINING STAR

JIGNA PATEL

Cut, staple, glue, hang, smile! Cut, staple, glue, hang, smile! Cut, staple, glue, hang, smile! It is addictive, how many Shining Stars will you make?

[
Over Christmas as much as 83km² of wrapping paper will end up in UK rubbish bins, enough to cover an area larger than Guernsey.
]

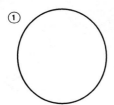

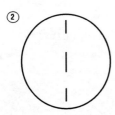

SHINING STAR

Skill Level
●●○○○

Time
30 min

YOU WILL NEED

Tools: Pencil, Compass (or jar lid to draw around), Scissors, String, Stapler, Glue

Materials: Scrap paper, Other decorative bits

HOW TO MAKE

1 Draw 14 circles the same size.

2 Fold all the circles in half and cut along the dotted line to get two semicircles.

3 Fold each of the 28 semicircles in half and staple at point x.

4 Glue together 14 of the semicircles to form the inner star.

5 Then glue 14 more semicircles into each of the gaps.

6 Then decorate the star as you wish.

7 Once done sew a string through one side and hang.

SNOWBALL POMPOMS
BARLEY MASSEY

A thrifty update on a classic these plastic bag snow-ball pompoms will come out year after year. And once you get in the pompom making mood who knows where you'll go with it. Scarves, jewellery, bobble that hat! This is one that could keep you gently productive on a winter's evening in front of the box.

[
I am passionate about passing on my textile skills and approach to recycling to others. We need to keep passing on these skills and resourceful attitudes to the next generation and it's a lot of fun!
]

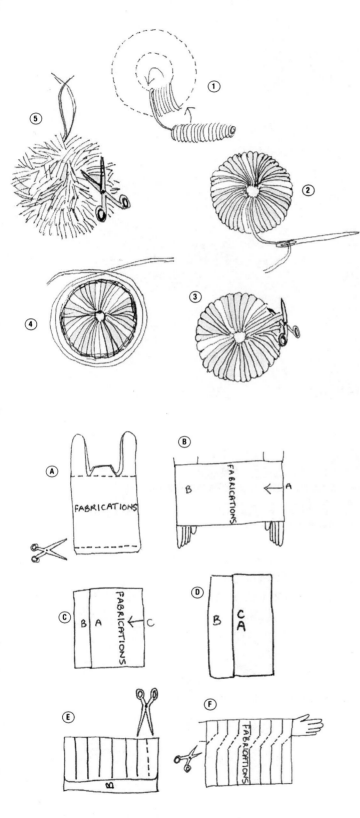

SNOWBALL POMPOMS

Skill Level	Time
●○○○○	30 min

YOU WILL NEED

Tools: Pencil, Scissors, Darning needle

Materials: White plastic bags, Glittery yarn to mix in (optional), Cardboard (cereal boxes work well), Large coin, Jar lid

HOW TO MAKE

1 Create a cardboard ring by drawing and cutting around a jar lid and coin. The diameter of the ring will determine the size of your Snowball Pompom. Cut up your plastic bag (as per clever instructions below for plastic bag yarn steps A-F) and wind into thin bullet shapes that will get through the central hole easily.

2 Wrap yarn around the disc until it is full (you can use a darning needle once the hole gets tight).

3 Holding onto the plastic bag yarn wrapped around the disc, cut through the layers, making sure that every layer is cut through.

4 Now wrap a double length of white yarn or thin string around the middle and double knot tightly together. This secures all the cut strips in place and doubles up as a hanging loop.

5 Remove the cardboard ring and give your Snowball Pompom a haircut to tidy off any loose ends. Hang it up and admire!

(A) Flatten out the plastic bag on a flat surface. Cut off the bottom seam and the handles.

(B) Place your hands through the cut open edges and open out into a rectangular tube. Flatten out the bag again.

(C) Fold point A (NB: the uncut edge) to point B (leaving about 3" from the other uncut edge) Now fold point C to point B.

(D) Cut strips (about 2" wide) through the folds A + C to point B. CAUTION! Do not cut all the way!

(E) Open the bag to reveal several rings of plastic. Place your arm through the rings to show uncut gap.

(F) Cut diagonally from the edge to the first cut, and then continue as in diagram to create a continuous length of plastic bag yarn.

UPLOAD YOUR CREATIONS TO WWW.REDESIGNDESIGN.ORG/GALLERY

SOCK ALIENS
LIZZIE LEE

Lizzie Lee's Sock Aliens are from another planet! If you don't a get chance to make some before Christmas, you might just find that this design makes good use of the novelty gift socks you are sometimes given but never wear.

[
Make a lonely sock happy this Christmas!
]

SOCK ALIENS

Skill Level ●●○○○   **Time** 1 hour

YOU WILL NEED

Tools: Needle and thread, Scissors

Materials: Socks, Fabric stuffing, Odd buttons

HOW TO MAKE

1 Lay your sock flat with the heel part at the front. Fold the heel part to form a tongue.

2 Cut the top part of this or another sock off to make the lips.

3 Place this piece around the tongue to form the mouth.

4 Using running stitch, stitch through both layers of lips and the tongue from one side to the other as low down as you can.

5 You can leave your alien's lips like this or you can fold the lips back and secure them to the sock using overstitch. It is best to put one hand in the sock when you do this, to prevent you from stitching through both sides of the sock.

6 How many legs is your alien going to have? It could have none or 2 or 3 or 4. mine has 2. With the sock laid flat carefully cut through both sides to the length you want the legs.

7 Stuff your alien up to the top of the legs - pushing the stuffing into the top of the head.

8 Starting at the bottom of one leg, stitch in over-stitch up to the top of the leg and down the next, leaving the bottoms of the legs open for stuffing. If you have 3 legs, you'll have to do this twice or 4 legs - 3 times. Stuff the legs and stitch across the bottoms of the legs in over-stitch.

9 How many eyes will your alien have? Securing your thread in the sock, stitch up through the button and back down at least 5 times, stitching through the sock behind the button each time.

TIP: Check out Lizzie's Sock Alien Gallery at www.remake.me.uk for inspiration.

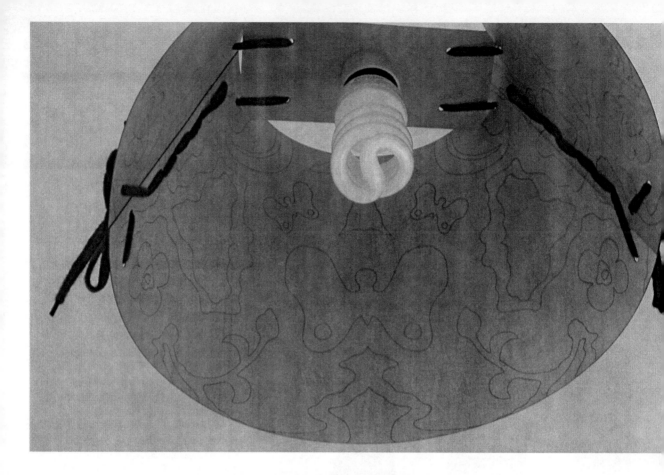

SOCRAFTY
SPINIFEX

This cardboard shade uses shoelaces as a clever decorative joining mechanism. SOcrafty is a lovely project to personalise using your own photos, paper cut outs and drawings.

[
The SOcrafty light shade is a nice simple, self-assembly, glueless, three-part construction, that is neatly held together with two shoelaces.
]

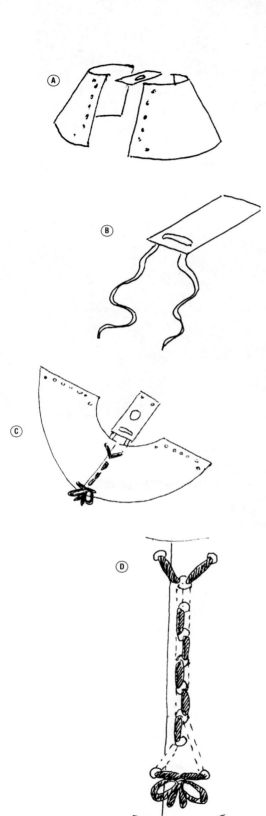

SOCRAFTY

Skill Level	Time	Template
●●●○○	1 hour	Page 91

YOU WILL NEED

Tools: Scissors or Craft knife, Ruler, Pencil, Hole punch

Materials: 1 Pair 100cm shoelaces, 2 Sheets A2 thick paper or card, 1 Sheet A4 corrugated card (fluting running length ways)

Health and Safety: The shade is only for use with energy saving bulbs. Switch off the light before attaching shade.

HOW TO MAKE

1 Using the shade panel template mark out and cut the parts from your selected thick paper or card.

2 Using the bulb holder strip template mark out and cut the part from the corrugated card. Ensure the fluting runs along the length of the strip.

3 Using the templates mark and cut out the holes where required.

4 The basic structure of the shade has the two shade panels curved around and held with a shoelace on each side. The strip (also held with the laces) spans the opening at the top across the centre. Ⓐ

5 Start by threading the shoelace through the two holes on one side of the strip. Ensure equal lengths of lace are left on each side. Ⓑ

6 Overlap the holes of the two shade panels and lace together one side of the shade with the shoelace attached to the strip Ⓒ The diagram is only a suggested method. Ⓓ Feel free to invent your own! Tie it off in a bow.

7 Bend the two panels of the shade around until the remaining holes align. Now repeat this process with the second shoelace.

TIP: Why not use your spare wrapping paper to decorate inside the shade?

TABLE WINE
LULA DOT

Wine bottles plus wood equals table - what a great piece of occasional furniture, and most apt! You could even paint it and hang it on the wall out of the way, ready to swing into action when your Christmas party guests arrive.

[A fantastic use for your Christmas waste.]

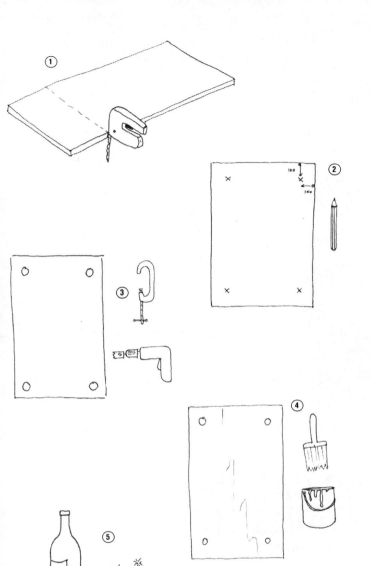

TABLE WINE

Skill Level
● ● ● ● ○

Time
1 hour

YOU WILL NEED

Tools: Drill, 32mm Hole drill bit, Paintbrush, Clamps, Tape measure or Ruler, Pencil, Jigsaw or handsaw (if wood needs to be cut to size)

Materials: 4 Wine bottles, Wood or old wooden table top, Varnish or Paint

HOW TO MAKE

1 Select and cut wood to desired size, or reclaim old coffee table top.

2 Mark an x in each corner 100mm in from the sides.

3 Clamp wood and drill four 32mm holes. Keep drill straight!

4 Varnish or Paint.

5 Drink four bottles of wine, preferably all of the same bottle type (not necessarily all at once!) and rinse out.

6 Push bottle necks through holes.

7 You now have a coffee table with candle holders and or flower vases in every corner!

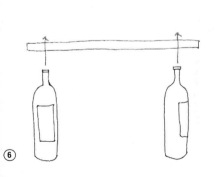

TREES CAN BE MOUNTAINS TOO

A SECRET CLUB

Schhh! Don't tell anyone else but Kenn Munk from a secret club makes lots of fabulous paper craft stuff. Make his clever cone tree and mountain your own by adding a splash of colour. For more inspiring design visit www.schhh.org

[
12.5 million tons of paper and cardboard are used annually in the UK
]

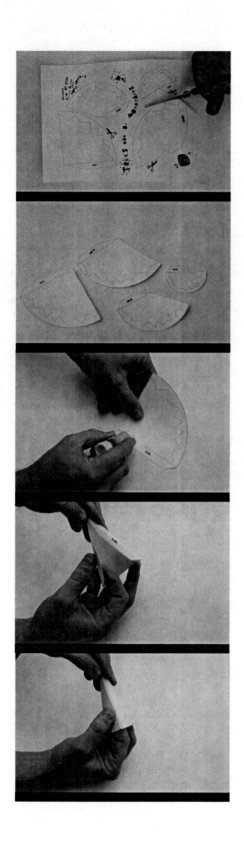

TREES CAN BE MOUNTAINS TOO

Skill Level	Time	Template
●○○○○	30 min	Page 93

YOU WILL NEED

Tools: Craft knife or Scissors, Glue stick

Materials: Paper, Crayons, pens to decorate (optional)

HOW TO MAKE

1 Cut out using craft knife or scissors.

2 Roll into cones.

3 Glue the tabs.

4 Place either side by side…

5 Or stacked as a tree. (Optional: You can decorate as you wish before gluing).

TIP: Repeat to create mountain ranges or forests!

WOOLLY
KITO COLCHESTER

We love a bit of kitchen chemistry so find this is very exciting – an invitation to cook up bio-plastic in the kitchen and make quirky lampshades out of old jumpers. Nice, very nice.

[Woolly is an eco-friendly lamp made from reclaimed textile and a bio-plastic that can be cooked up in the kitchen! The design is flexible and can be modified to suit, allowing you to take inspiration from household objects and use them as moulds.]

WOOLLY

Skill Level
●●●○○

Time
4 hours

YOU WILL NEED

Tools: Mould (a bucket, a bottle, anything you like actually!), Hob, Wooden spoon, Saucepan, Scissors

Materials: Old jumper, Cooking oil, Starch (corn, potato, rice, etc.), Vinegar, Clingfilm (if you are using a metal mould)

Health and Safety: The shade is only for use with energy saving bulbs. Switch off the light before attaching shade.

HOW TO MAKE

1 Mix bio-plastic ingredients in a saucepan - Recipe: 14 parts water, 3 parts starch, 2 parts vinegar.

2 Heat until it forms a consistent goo.

3 Allow to cool.

4 Cut off jumper sleeve.

5 Work bio-plastic into the jumper sleeve until the fabric is saturated.

6 Apply oil to mould. If your mould is metal use clingfilm first to prevent sticking.

7 Stretch sleeve over mould.

8 Allow to dry for one to four days depending on fabric and climate.

9 Remove from mould and cut to desired shape.

TIPS:

Make sure that the wool is completely saturated with bio-plastic as this will ensure that the form is rigid when dry.

To speed up the cooling process after heating the mixture place the saucepan in a larger one half filled with cold water.

Lampshade is secured to cable with a clothes peg.

WOOLLY CHAINS
BARLEY MASSEY

Make your own French knitting tool then make your own French knitting. Aren't you clever! If you've more time and wool on your hands once you're done making Woolly Chains, you'll find French knitting is a fantastic way to make a Dr Who scarf (you know, the real Dr Who from the 70s!).

[Craft is very sociable! Craft is ideal for community cohesion! Craft is great for family learning! In short Craft rocks!]

WOOLLY CHAINS

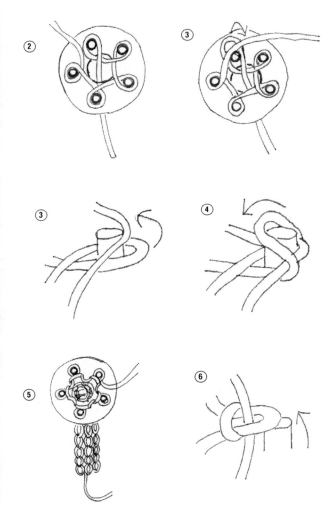

Skill Level
●●○○○

Time
1 hour /Chain

YOU WILL NEED

Tools: Scissors

Materials: Map pins with long coloured heads (or nails*), Wooden curtain ring (or bobbin*), Salvaged wool, Odd balls and ends in a variety of colours

HOW TO MAKE

1 To create the chains you will be French knitting either on your own homemade Nelly or on one from Barley's shop - Fabrications (www.fabrications1.co.uk).

To make your own simply put at least 5 map pins into a curtain ring equal distance apart *(if you can find a wooden cotton bobbin you can put nails around the top and make a Nelly as it was done in the good old days).

2 To start knitting pass the end of the wool through the central hole, leaving enough to hold and secure. With the other end wrap the wool to the right of the first pin and around the back, creating a half figure of eight. Continue around all the other pins until you are back where you started.

3 Now you're ready to start knitting! Pass the wool behind the pin, above the first loop.

4 Lift the loop over, creating your first stitch.

5 Continue going round and around each pin in the same way keeping it nice and loose to create a tube of knitting until it's the length you wish your first woolly chain link to be.

6 To cast off pass the wool through each loop to secure and stop it unravelling. Cut off leaving a tail to knot to other end of the tube creating your chain link.

For the next chain repeat the knitting and thread through the link and tie off as before and watch your chain grow!

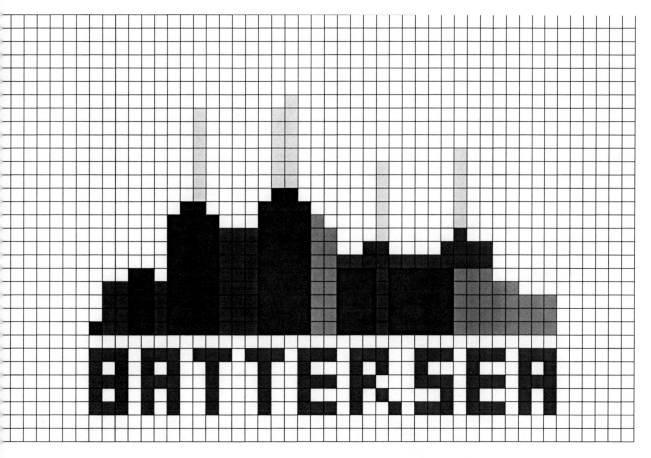

Anchor thread colours

1080
◻ *very light brown*

1008
▨ *light brown/orange*

904
◼ *rich brown*

382
◼ *dark brown/grey*

Battersea Power Station Cross Stitch Make Industries - found on page 10

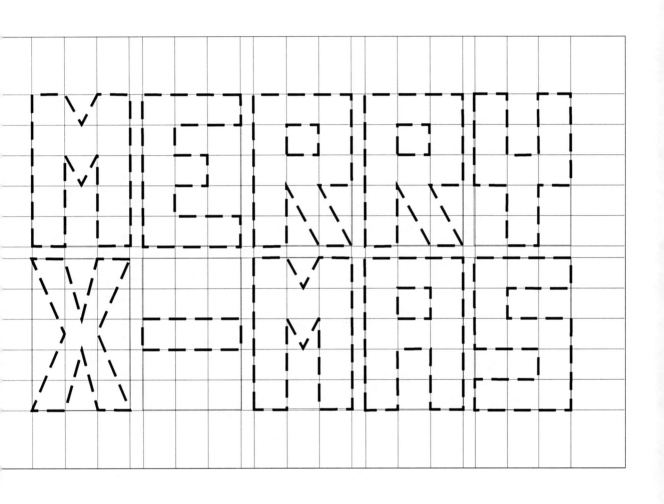

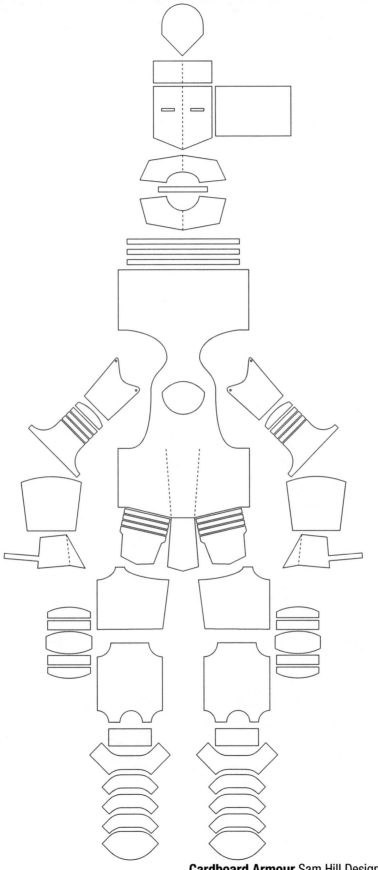

Cardboard Armour Sam Hill Design - found on page 22

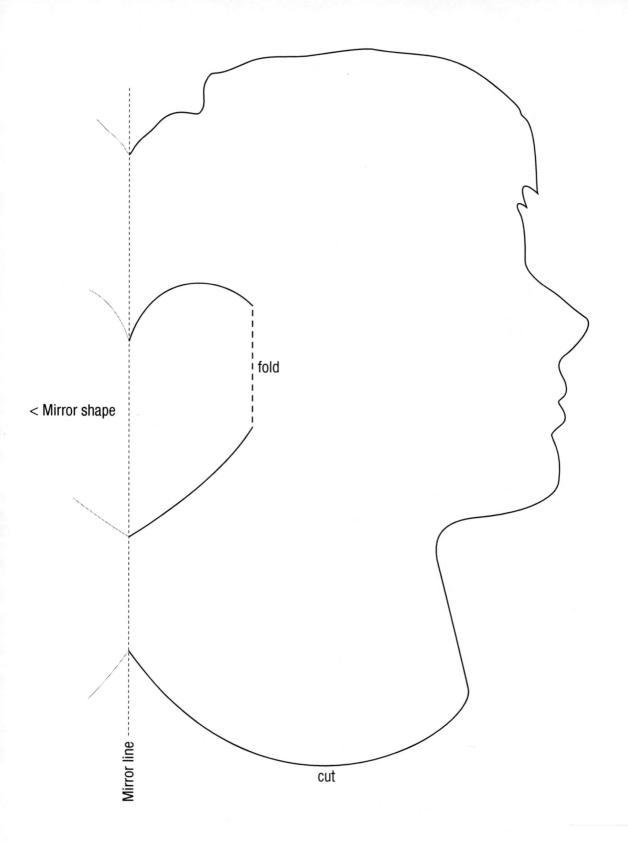

< Mirror shape

fold

cut

Mirror line

My Profile Lamp Rada Lewis - found on page 40

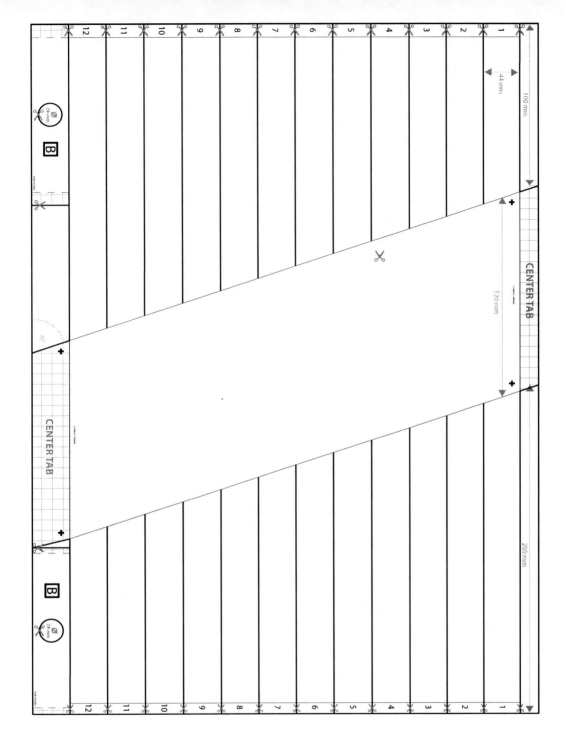

KEY

Reference line	————————
Fold line	— — — —
Cut line	▬▬▬▬▬▬

s template is **1:10 Scale.**

arge this template to **correct scale** before use or download
print it from www.redesigndesign.org/whydontyou

ase use only **Max 11W** low energy bulb.

Octopus Illuminati Arash & Kelly - found on page 42

Pixel-It grid (for 76mmx76mm Post-It Notes)

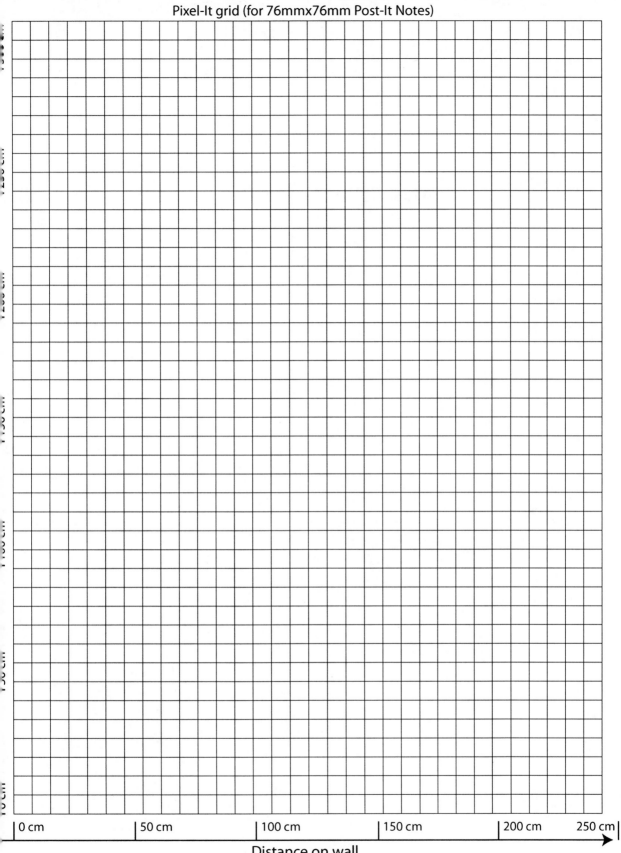

0 cm   50 cm   100 cm   150 cm   200 cm   250 cm

Distance on wall

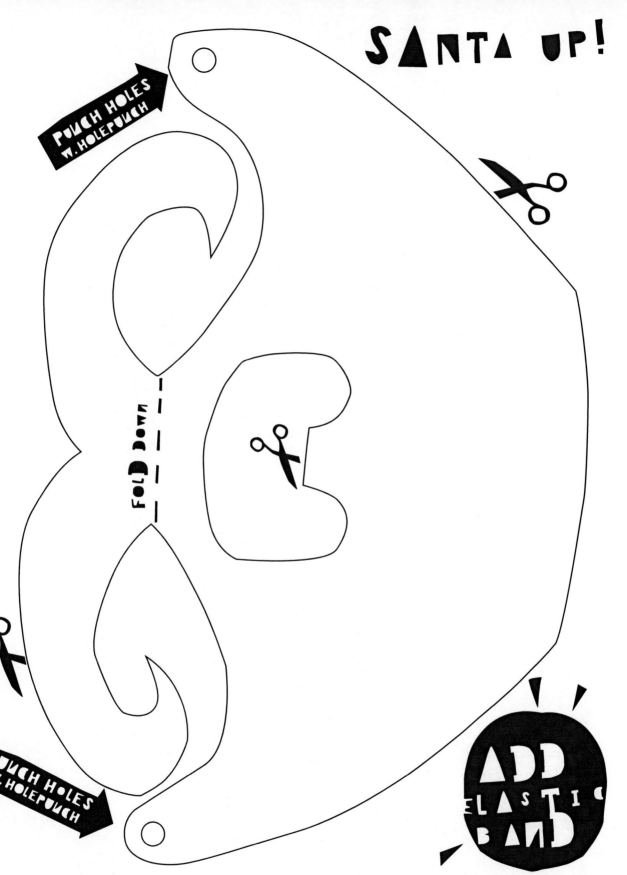

Santa up! A Secret Club - found on page 56

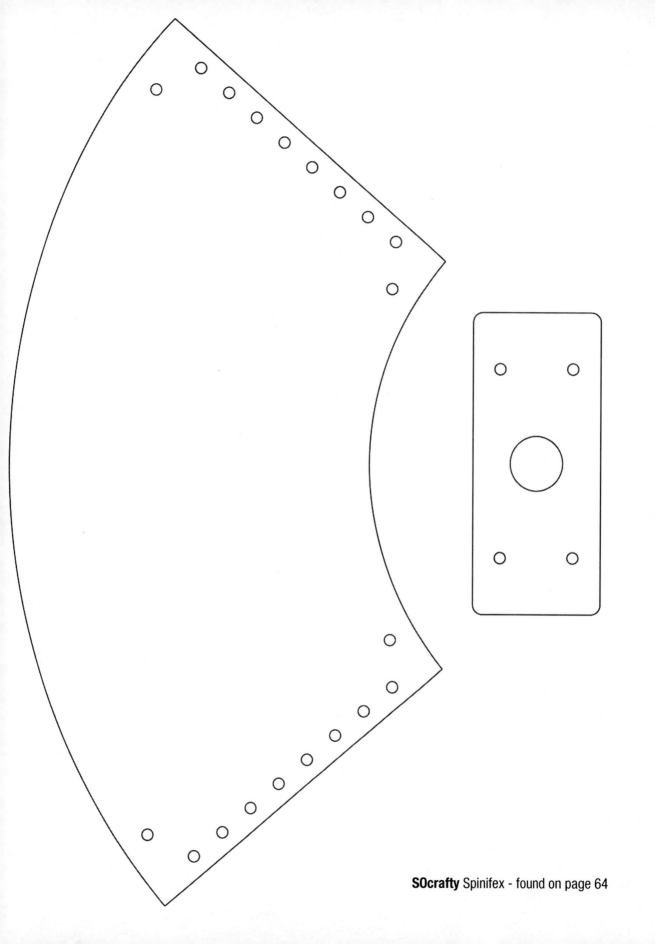

SOcrafty Spinifex - found on page 64

ARRANGE SIDE BY SIDE TO MAKE A RANGE OF MOUNTAINS

GLUE

GLUE

TREES CAN BE MOUNTAINS TOO

STACK TO MAKE TREES

GLUE

GLUE

Trees can be mountains too A Secret Club - found on page 68

BALLOON BOWLS
GITTA GSCHWENDTNER

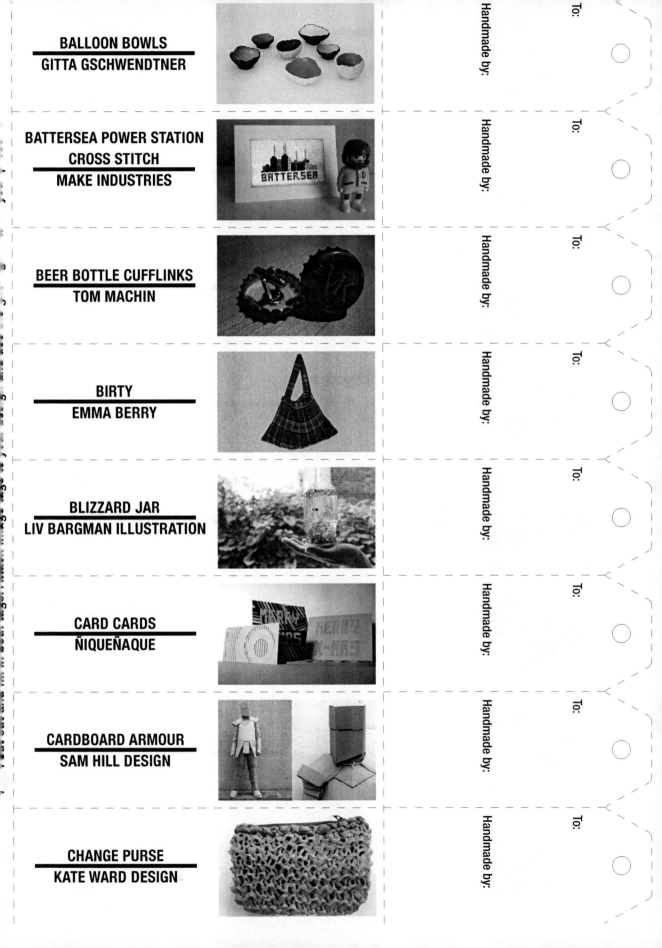

To:

Handmade by:

**BATTERSEA POWER STATION
CROSS STITCH**
MAKE INDUSTRIES

To:

Handmade by:

BEER BOTTLE CUFFLINKS
TOM MACHIN

To:

Handmade by:

BIRTY
EMMA BERRY

To:

Handmade by:

BLIZZARD JAR
LIV BARGMAN ILLUSTRATION

To:

Handmade by:

CARD CARDS
ÑIQUEÑAQUE

To:

Handmade by:

CARDBOARD ARMOUR
SAM HILL DESIGN

To:

Handmade by:

CHANGE PURSE
KATE WARD DESIGN

To:

Handmade by:

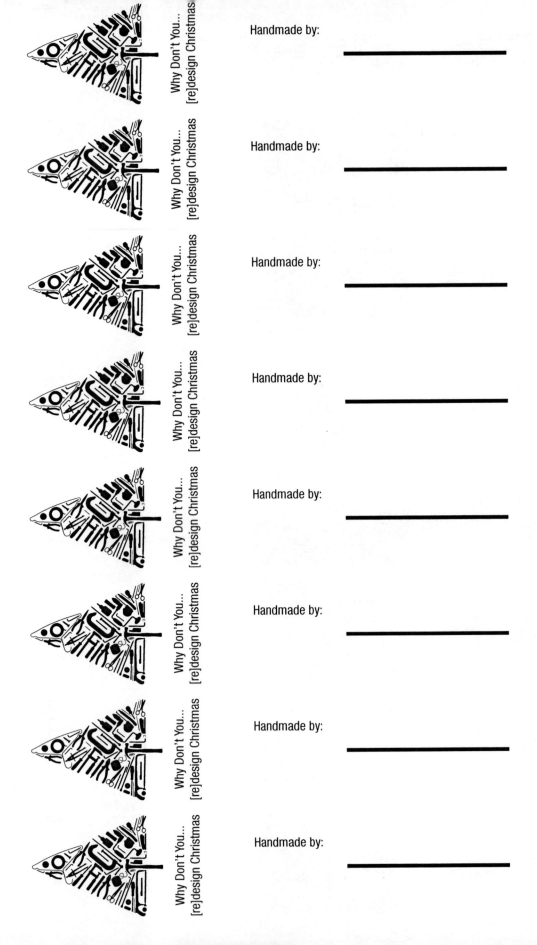

Why Don't You…
[re]design Christmas

Handmade by:

Why Don't You…
[re]design Christmas

Handmade by:

Why Don't You…
[re]design Christmas

Handmade by:

Why Don't You…
[re]design Christmas

Handmade by:

Why Don't You…
[re]design Christmas

Handmade by:

Why Don't You…
[re]design Christmas

Handmade by:

Why Don't You…
[re]design Christmas

Handmade by:

Why Don't You…
[re]design Christmas

Handmade by:

CHESTNUT ANTLERS
(FOR MATHILDA)
DUNCAN KRAMER

To:

Handmade by:

CHRISTMAS COMFORT
LULA DOT

To:

Handmade by:

EDIBLE DECORATIONS
ANTHONY DICKENS DESIGN

To:

Handmade by:

FILIGREE FANTASY
PHIONA RICHARDS

To:

Handmade by:

IWIRE
SANJAY KATIYAR

To:

Handmade by:

KILIKANZER
ANTIGOR

To:

Handmade by:

LOVELY AND QUIET MUGS
SUGRU

To:

Handmade by:

MIMO
WEMAKE

To:

Handmade by:

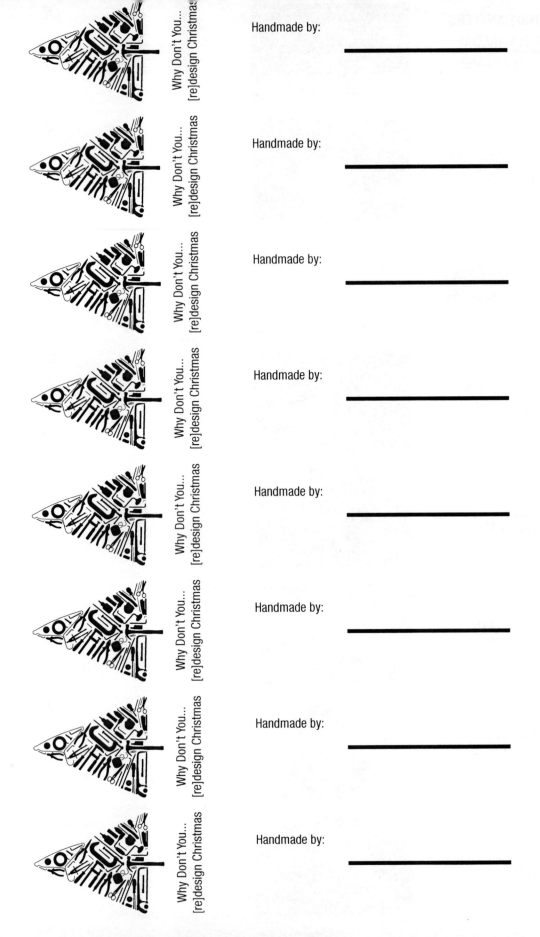

Why Don't You... [re]design Christmas

Handmade by:

Why Don't You... [re]design Christmas

Handmade by:

Why Don't You... [re]design Christmas

Handmade by:

Why Don't You... [re]design Christmas

Handmade by:

Why Don't You... [re]design Christmas

Handmade by:

Why Don't You... [re]design Christmas

Handmade by:

Why Don't You... [re]design Christmas

Handmade by:

Why Don't You... [re]design Christmas

Handmade by:

MY PROFILE LAMP
RADA LEWIS

OCTOPUS ILLUMINATI
ARASH AND KELLY

ODD SOCK TOY
EMMA BERRY

PALLET STOOL
STUDIOMAMA

PIXEL-IT
OLIVER BISHOP-YOUNG

RECYCLED PLASTIC BAG
CHRISTMAS WREATH
GIRLWITHBEADS

RECYCLED PLASTIC
LACE LAMPSHADE
KATE WARD DESIGN

SANTA UP!
A SECRET CLUB

To: .... Handmade by:

To: .... Handmade by:

To: .... Handmade by:

To: .... Handmade by:

To: .... Handmade by:

To: .... Handmade by:

To: .... Handmade by:

To: .... Handmade by:

Why Don't You...
[re]design Christmas

Handmade by:

Why Don't You...
[re]design Christmas

Handmade by:

Why Don't You...
[re]design Christmas

Handmade by:

Why Don't You...
[re]design Christmas

Handmade by:

Why Don't You...
[re]design Christmas

Handmade by:

Why Don't You...
[re]design Christmas

Handmade by:

Why Don't You...
[re]design Christmas

Handmade by:

Why Don't You...
[re]design Christmas

Handmade by:

SHINING STARS
JIGNA PATEL

To:

Handmade by:

SNOWBALL POM POMS
BARLEY MASSEY

To:

Handmade by:

SOCK ALIENS
LIZZIE LEE

To:

Handmade by:

SOCRAFTY
SPINIFEX

To:

Handmade by:

TABLE WINE
LULA DOT

To:

Handmade by:

TREES CAN BE
MOUNTAINS TOO
A SECRET CLUB

To:

Handmade by:

WOOLLY
KULTURLABOR TRIAL
& ERROR

To:

Handmade by:

WOOLLY CHAINS
BARLEY MASSEY

To:

Handmade by:

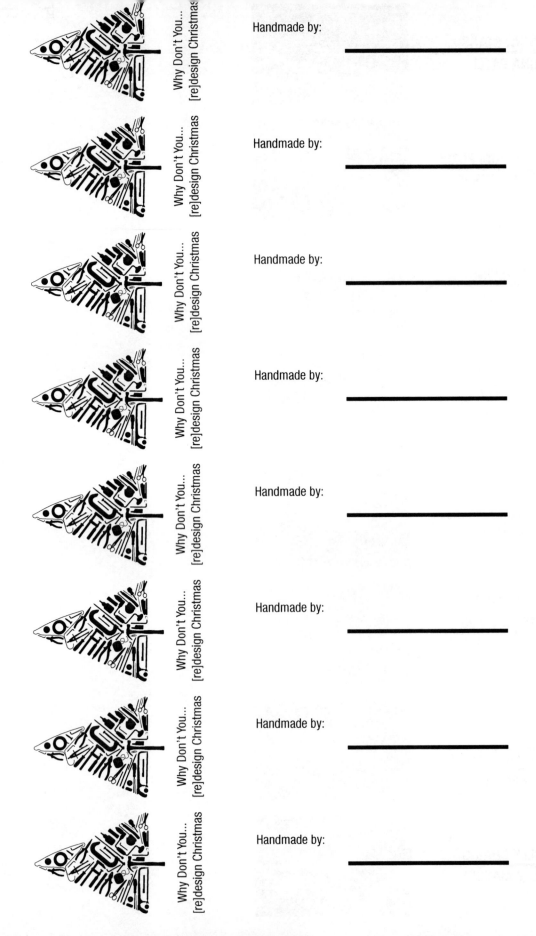

Why Don't You...
[re]design Christmas

Handmade by:

Why Don't You...
[re]design Christmas

Handmade by:

Why Don't You...
[re]design Christmas

Handmade by:

Why Don't You...
[re]design Christmas

Handmade by:

Why Don't You...
[re]design Christmas

Handmade by:

Why Don't You...
[re]design Christmas

Handmade by:

Why Don't You...
[re]design Christmas

Handmade by:

Why Don't You...
[re]design Christmas

Handmade by:

I MADE THIS

MIY PROJECT	HANDMADE BY	ADDED TO GALLERY WWW.REDESIGNDESGN.ORG/GALLERY	DATE

DESIGNERS DIRECTORY

A Secret Club
info@kennmunk.com
www.schhh.org

Anthony Dickens Design
studio@anthonydickens.com
www.anthonydickens.com

Antigor
antigor2002@yahoo.co.uk

Arash and Kelly
studio@arashandkelly.com
www.arashandkelly.com

Barley Massey
barley@fabrications1.co.uk
www.fabrications1.co.uk

Emma Berry
made@makingmatters.com
www.makingmatters.com

Duncan Kramer / FYC
info@frontyardcompany.co.uk
www.frontyardcompany.co.uk

girlwithbeads
girl@girlwithbeads.co.uk
www.girlwithbeads.co.uk

Gitta Gschwendtner
mail@gittagschwendtner.com
www.gittagschwendtner.com

Jigna Patel
jigna.r.patel@hotmail.com

Kate Ward Design
kate.r.ward@gmail.com
www.kateward.com.au

Kulturlabor Trial & Error
Kito@carrot.com
www.kitocolchester.co.uk
www.trial-error.org

Liv Bargman Illustration
info@livbargman.co.uk
www.livbargman.co.uk

Lizzie Lee
lizzielee@another.com
www.lizzielee.com
www.remake.me.uk

Lula Dot
design@luladot.com
www.luladot.com

Make Industries
mail@makeindustries.co.uk
www.makeindustries.co.uk

[re]design
info@redesigndesign.org
www.redesigndesign.org

sugru
jane@sugru.com
www.sugru.com

Ñiqueñaque
emma@cyclefabric.co.uk
www.cyclefabric.co.uk

Sam Hill Design
contact@samhilldesign.com
www.samhilldesign.com

Tina Dhingra
tinadhingra@gmail.com
www.plantedlog.wordpress.com

Oliver Bishop-Young
olly@oliverbishopyoung.co.uk
www.oliverbishopyoung.co.uk

Sanjay Katiyar
s.katiyar@hotmail.co.uk
www.sanjaykatiyar.com

Tom Machin
info@tommachin.co.uk
www.tommachin.com

Phiona Richards
rarenotions@hotmail.co.uk
www.rarenotions.co.uk

Spinifex
samm@spinifex.co.uk
www.spinifex.co.uk

WEmake
info@wemake.co.uk
www.wemake.co.uk

Rada Lewis
rada.lewis@gmail.com
www.radalewis.com
www. cargocollective.com/radalewis

Studiomama
tolstrup@studiomama.com
www.studiomama.com

[re]design is social enterprise that encourages sustainable actions through design. We partner with a wide range of organisations to pioneer strategic approaches to sustainable design.

As climate change demonstrates the urgency of sustainable behaviour change, [re]design sets out to decouple eco-awareness from doom and gloom. The need for sustainable design is an opportunity to ask how we can create true quality of life; now and for the future.

[RE]DESIGN - OTHER PUBLICATIONS

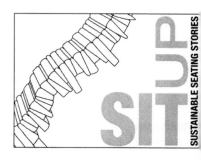

DOING IT FOR THE KIDS
ISBN 978-0-9557129-2-0

From a teddy made from a placenta to footballs made from relief aid packaging, Doing It For The Kids uncovers the latest amazing, innovative ideas in sustainable toy design today. Illustrated with fun design-based activities, it's a must read, must-do book for big kids and little kids everywhere.

LIGHTEN UP
ISBN 978-0-9557129-1-3

Lighten Up is an illuminating exploration of switched-on domestic lighting solutions from the UK. The quest for sustainability is driving the evolution of new technologies, aesthetics, materials and interactions. Shedding light on the stories behind the products, Lighten Up offers insight and inspiration for the next generation of lighting.

SIT UP
ISBN 978-0-9557129-0-6

Are you sitting comfortably? And sustainably? SIT UP gets to the bottom of sixteen "good" and gorgeous seats from UK designers with a passion for sustainability.

Lightning Source UK Ltd.
Milton Keynes UK
27 October 2010

161930UK00001B/16/P